What does it mean to have

Epilepsy

Louise Spilsbury

Heinemann
LIBRARY

www.heinemann.co.uk/library
Visit our website to find out more information about Heinemann Library books.

To order:
☎ Phone 44 (0) 1865 888066
▤ Send a fax to 44 (0) 1865 314091
💻 Visit the Heinemann Bookshop at www.heinemann.co.uk/library to browse our
catalogue and order online.

First published in Great Britain by Heinemann Library,
Halley Court, Jordan Hill, Oxford OX2 8EJ,
a division of Reed Educational and Professional Publishing Ltd.
Heinemann is a registered trademark of Reed Educational and Professional Publishing Ltd.

OXFORD MELBOURNE AUCKLAND
JOHANNESBURG BLANTYRE GABORONE
IBADAN PORTSMOUTH (NH) USA CHICAGO

Designed by AMR
Illustrated by David Woodroffe
Originated by Dot Gradations
Printed in China by Wing King Tong

ISBN 0 431 13934 2 (hardback)   ISBN 0 431 13941 5 (paperback)
07 06 05 04 03 02   08 07 06 05 04 03
10 9 8 7 6 5 4 3 2 1   10 9 8 7 6 5 4 3 2 1

British Library Cataloguing in Publication Data
Spilsbury, Louise
  What does it mean to have epilepsy?
  1.Epilepsy – Juvenile literature
  I.Title II.Epilepsy
  616.8'53

Acknowledgements
The publishers would like to thank the following for permission to reproduce photographs: Gareth Boden:
pp.8, 9, 12, 13, 16, 17, 20, 21, 22, 26, 28, 29; Bubbles/Angela Hampton: p.27; Sally and Richard
Greenhill: pp.5, 14, 23, 24; Medipics/Dan McCoy: pp.4, 15; Pymca: p.19; Science Photo Library: p.11;
Science Photo Library/Saturn Stills: p.10; Stone: p.18; Wellcome Photo Library/Anthea Siveking: p.25.

The pictures on the following pages were posed by models who do not have epilepsy: pp.12, 13, 28, 29.

Special thanks to: Beryl and Shaun.

The publishers would also like to thank the National Centre for Young People With Epilepsy and Julie
Johnson, PHSE Consultant Trainer and Writer, for their help in the preparation of this book.

Cover photograph reproduced with permission of Sally and Richard Greenhill.

Every effort has been made to contact copyright holders of any material   ook.
Any omissions will be rectified in subseq

Contents

What is epilepsy? 4

What causes seizures? 6

What are seizures like? 8

Identifying epilepsy 10

Meet Rowan 12

Controlling epilepsy 14

Taking medicine 16

Tackling the triggers 18

Meet Beryl and Shaun 20

Living with epilepsy 22

At school 24

At home 26

Meet Ellen 28

Glossary 30

Helpful books and addresses 31

Index 32

Any words appearing in the text in bold, **like this**, are explained in the Glossary.

What is epilepsy?

The word epilepsy comes from the Greek word 'epilambanein', which means 'to seize'. If someone in your school has epilepsy, it means they have a tendency to have **seizures**.

Even though epilepsy is quite a common **condition**, you don't see many people having seizures. This is because most people who have epilepsy take medicines which stop or greatly reduce the number of seizures they have. This means that most young people who have epilepsy are able to do the things their friends do – from swimming to skateboarding, dancing to diving!

Epilepsy facts
- Epilepsy affects people all over the world. It can affect anyone of any age, although half of all people with epilepsy develop it before they are ten years old.
- On average, one person in twenty people will have a seizure in their lifetime, perhaps after a shock or if they have a high temperature. The difference is that people who have epilepsy have repeated seizures.
- About one person in 200 people has epilepsy.

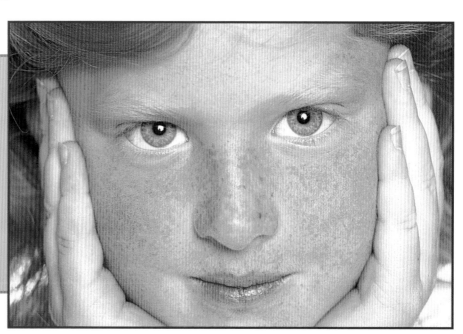

People with epilepsy are just like anyone else, except they have a tendency to have seizures.

Most people with epilepsy take medicine to stop or reduce the number of seizures they have, leaving them to get on with doing the things they enjoy.

People who have seizures may have them often, or only once in a while. There are many different kinds of epileptic seizures. For example, when some people have seizures they simply seem to drift off – they sit very still and stare into space, as if they are daydreaming. Others may become **unconscious** for a few moments and, if they are not sitting down at the time, they may fall down.

If you see someone having a seizure, you might feel worried about them. In fact, seizures themselves don't hurt people, but there is a danger that people may knock or injure themselves while having one. Most seizures last only a matter of seconds or minutes and, although some people feel a little tired or have a slight headache afterwards, most don't remember anything about them. After a rest, they usually get right back to what they were doing before.

What causes seizures?

A **seizure** is caused by a temporary (short-term) change in the way **nerve cells** in the **brain** work. You need to know a bit about the brain to understand what this means. Your brain is the control centre of your body. It controls the other parts of the body and ensures that they all work properly together.

The brain is connected to the rest of your body by **nerves**. Nerves are a bit like telephone lines. Messages from all parts of your body travel along the nerves to the **spinal cord** (inside your backbone) and up to the brain. Messages from the brain travel to the spinal cord and on to other parts of the body. So if you touch something hot, **nerve endings** in your hand send a pain message to your brain. The brain sends an urgent message to tell you to move your hand – quickly! Messages such as these travel around your body and through the brain at lightning speed.

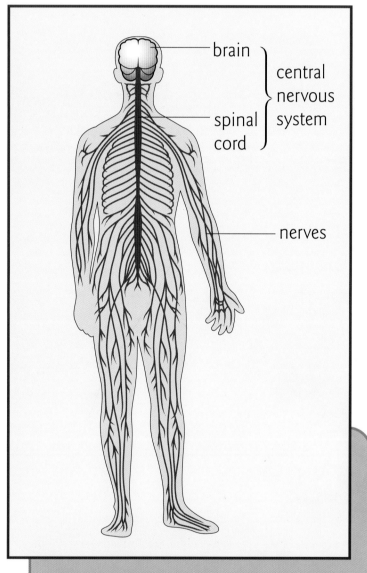

brain

central nervous system

spinal cord

nerves

Your brain sends messages to, and receives messages from, the rest of your body along a network of nerves.

Nerve cells at work!

The brain is like a living computer, but one that is more powerful and subtle than any machine. It deals with a huge range of complicated tasks and instructions. It is made up of millions of nerve cells. Different clusters (groups) of nerve cells make up different parts of the brain. These parts deal with different kinds of messages. For example, some parts respond to signals from your senses; others help you to move around in a controlled way.

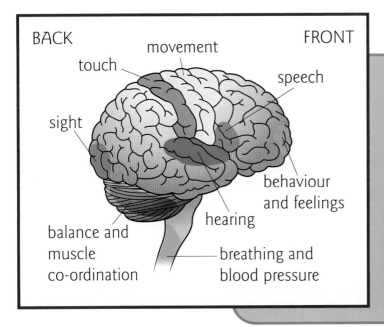

BACK

FRONT

movement

touch

speech

sight

behaviour
and feelings

hearing

balance and
muscle
co-ordination

breathing and
blood pressure

Different parts of the brain are responsible for different jobs in the body. Nerve cells in each part of the brain work together and also with nerve cells in the other parts.

When seizures happen

The nerve cells in the brain pass messages to each other as **electrical signals**. Usually, these signals travel without a hitch. Once in a while, in people with epilepsy, a set of nerve cells sends bursts of electrical signals that are mixed up and move much faster than usual. This affects normal activity in that part of the brain and causes a change in the way the person behaves – resulting in what we call a **seizure**.

What are seizures like?

Seizures happen when ordinary brain activity is suddenly disrupted – but what is it like to have a seizure? Because the brain is responsible for so many things – feelings, movements, memory and so on – any of these can be affected, depending upon what part of the brain is involved. Some people feel different when they have a seizure. They may suddenly feel scared, worried or confused. They may mumble, fumble with their clothes or even wander about. Others experience jerky, uncontrolled movements. Still others may go blank, not feeling or thinking about anything for a few seconds. Some people become **unconscious** when they have a seizure, so they feel nothing at all.

The kind and number of seizures someone has vary from person to person. Individuals who have epilepsy may also have different kinds of seizures at different times. Some people feel quite groggy for a while after a seizure, while others feel fine as soon as they come round.

Some people say their seizures can be a bit like watching a video when the screen suddenly goes blank. When it starts up again, they have no memory of how long it was off.

What to do when a seizure happens

Would you know what to do if you saw someone having a seizure? For some kinds of seizure you don't need to do anything at all. If someone is shaking a lot, or has fallen down or become unconscious, you should follow these simple steps.

1 Keep calm. Don't ever try to 'wake' the person up or hold them still, even if they are shaking.
2 Move any hard, sharp or hot objects out of the way to stop them hurting themselves.
3 Place a cushion or something soft, like a rolled-up jacket, under their head.
4 Ask people not to crowd around and never let anyone put anything, such as food or drink, in the person's mouth.
5 Try to time how long the seizure lasts.
6 Don't worry. The seizure will eventually stop. Wait quietly with them until they know where they are and what has happened. They might need to rest for a bit, but they should soon feel fine.

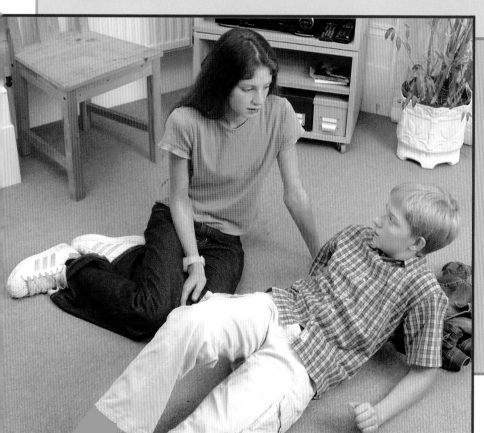

Seizures themselves don't cause people any pain and only last a few seconds or minutes. People need to see a doctor only if it is the first time they have had a seizure, if they hurt themselves or if the seizure lasts longer than five minutes.

Identifying epilepsy

It is not easy to tell if someone has epilepsy. Many people have a **seizure** at some point in their lives, perhaps when they are ill and have a very high temperature, or after a shock. Not all these people will develop epilepsy, so how do doctors decide if a person has it?

Doctors usually have to wait for the person to have other seizures and see what they are like. Because people who have seizures don't remember much about them, their family or friends give the doctor as full a picture as possible of what a seizure was like. This can help doctors decide whether or not someone really has epilepsy.

What causes epilepsy?

Sometimes it is obvious why someone has epilepsy. For example, in some people, seizures may start after an accident, perhaps when they fell out of a tree or off a horse and bumped their head badly. Sometimes children get epilepsy after a serious **infection**, such as **meningitis**, which affects the brain. For most people, however, doctors have no idea what causes it.

Doctors talk to the rest of the family to get a clear picture of what a child's seizures are like.

10

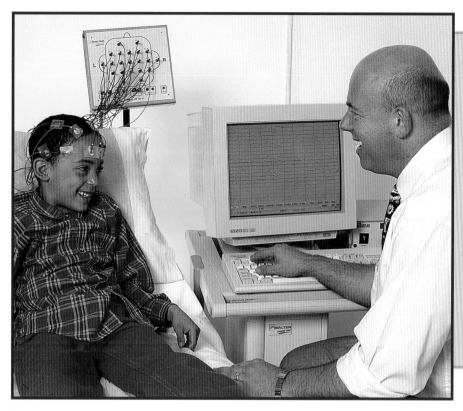

Having an EEG might sound and even look a bit daunting but, in fact, the test does not hurt a bit and many people are fascinated by what happens.

Tests

There are a number of tests doctors may use to help them **diagnose** epilepsy. One of these is a blood test. By checking a small sample of a person's blood, doctors can tell if the person is healthy and if they have a **condition** other than epilepsy that could be causing their seizures.

Some people also have an **EEG**. (This stands for electroencephalogram – you say 'electro-enkefalo-gram' – which is quite a mouthful!) This test measures the **electrical signals** coming from the brain's **nerve cells**. You sit or lie down and have about twenty little pads placed on your head. Doctors ask you to do different things, such as open and close your eyes or look at a flashing light, so they can see how your brain reacts. The pads pick up the electrical signals and copy them into a machine, which prints them onto paper as a series of wiggly lines. Doctors use these printouts to help them decide if you have epilepsy.

Meet Rowan

I'm Rowan and I'm ten years old. I live with my mum, my sister Rhiannon, who is twelve, and our two guinea pigs. I got epilepsy when I was seven years old. Rhiannon says that when she saw me have my first **seizure** it was a bit scary. We were in the garden and she says I just suddenly fell off the swing and started shaking. She thought I was just messing about but when she shouted at me I didn't seem to hear her, so she called our mum. Mum called the ambulance and went to hospital with me. Mum says that was when the doctors told her I might have epilepsy, but they couldn't tell for certain.

After that I had two more seizures quite close together, apparently. Mum and Rhiannon wrote down what happened. Mum's still got a page of her notes. It says: 'Rowan seemed to be fine when he suddenly cried out. Then he fell to the ground and started shaking. This lasted for 45 seconds. When he came round he didn't know where he was at first, and he said he felt a bit sick. He felt fine again after resting for five minutes.'

As well as reading Mum's notes, the doctors also asked me in for some tests. I don't remember any of the tests hurting and everyone at the hospital was really nice to me. Once they decided I really did have epilepsy, my doctor started me on some medicine. At first, it didn't help. In fact, it made me feel sick, so the doctor

tried me on a different sort. I have to take it two times a day, one in the morning after my cereal and one after tea. Mum bought me an alarm watch which goes off to remind me when to take the medicine, but she usually has it ready anyway.

When people find out I've got epilepsy, they look kind of worried. But it doesn't really bother me and it doesn't stop me doing what I want. I do loads of things. I do football training twice a week. I'm learning to play the flugelhorn (which the cats hate) and I've got a massive collection of joke books. At school, people think I'm a bit of a comedian, and I like being able to make the rest of the class laugh.

Controlling epilepsy

It is important to control epilepsy if you have it. Even though the **seizures** themselves don't cause pain, people may hurt themselves during a seizure, perhaps by falling down or bumping into something. As well as that, none of us likes to feel out of control. It can be upsetting to wake up in a room of people looking at you, with no idea of what you might have been doing or saying.

Most people who have epilepsy get the treatment they need to control their seizures, leaving them to enjoy normal activities.

The main way of controlling a person's epilepsy is with medicine. About four out of every five people who have epilepsy find that drugs (medicines) can stop or greatly reduce the number of seizures they have. Some people may also be able to reduce the number of seizures they have by avoiding the things that set them off, called **'triggers'**. Many people have seizures that happen for no apparent reason, but others find that they are more likely to have a seizure at certain times, perhaps when they are ill or overtired.

Keeping healthy

Many people believe that taking care of themselves can reduce the number or strength of the seizures they have. It is important for us all to look after our bodies if we want to stay healthy. We all feel better if we eat the right foods, including lots of fruit and vegetables, drink plenty of water, take plenty of rest as well as exercise and keep ourselves clean. **Stress** (worrying about things) also affects your health. We cannot avoid worrying about some things, and some stress is probably quite good for us, but try not to let it get out of hand. If something is worrying you a lot, talk it over with someone.

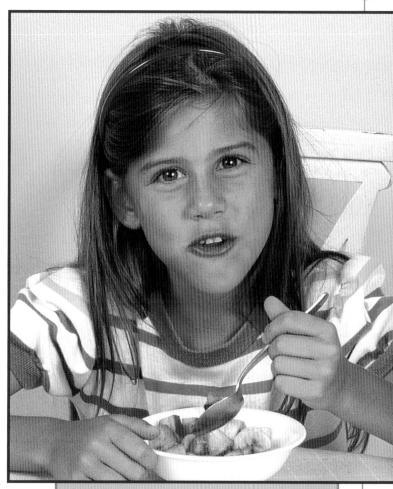

Eating a healthy diet is important for us all, including people who have epilepsy.

Growing up with epilepsy

If you have epilepsy, you may find that you get fewer seizures and that they become less serious as you get older. Some people even find that their seizures stop completely as they grow up. If this does not happen, there are medicines that can stop or reduce the seizures at all stages of your life.

Taking medicine

There are many different kinds of medicine for epilepsy and it can take a long time to find the one that is right for you. When a doctor has decided which one they think will suit you best, you try taking a small amount at first. This is to see if it works and to check that it does not have any **side-effects** (unwanted reactions), such as tiredness or finding it hard to concentrate. Eventually, people find a medicine that is right for them. People usually take their medicine in tablets, although very young children may have theirs as syrup.

Check-ups

If you have epilepsy you should visit your hospital or clinic every few months for a check-up. Doctors check that you are well and that the medicine you are taking is still right for you. When you are young, your body is growing and changing all the time, so the amount or kind of medicine you need to take might change, too.

The thought of having to take medicines every day might seem a bit annoying, but for most people it just becomes a part of their daily routine, like cleaning your teeth.

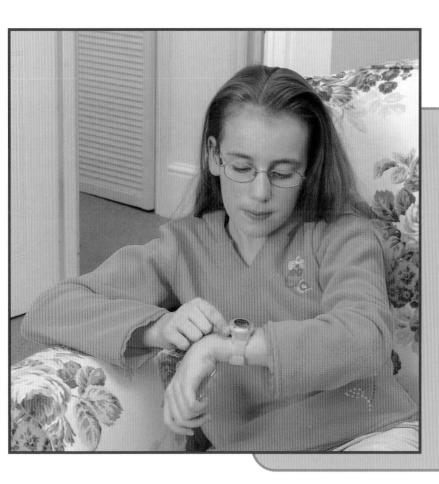

If you have epilepsy, it is important to take your medicine at the same time each day. Some people wear watches with built-in alarms to remind them when to take their tablets.

Tablet time

If you take drugs to control your epilepsy, it is really important that you take them at the times the doctor tells you to. Medicines for epilepsy only work if there is a constant balance of them in your body. If you miss a dose or take one at the wrong time, it can stop them from working properly.

If you take medicine for epilepsy, you probably have two doses a day, one after breakfast in the morning and the second after dinner in the evening. If you need to take a third dose, after lunch, you may need to ask a teacher to keep the tablets somewhere safe for you. Although the tablets are good for you, they could be harmful for someone else if they took them out of your bag and ate them by mistake, perhaps thinking they were sweets.

Tackling the triggers

Many people find that medicines stop them having any **seizures**. Others find that medicines help by reducing the number of seizures they have, but they don't stop completely. Most of these seizures strike out of the blue. You don't have any warning they are going to happen and there is nothing you do that seems to bring them on. Some people, though, find that there are certain factors that can bring on a seizure. Obviously, it is very useful to know what **triggers** (sets off) a seizure, if anything. That way you can try to avoid doing the things that bring on a seizure.

Keeping a trigger diary

Keeping a diary of your seizures is a good way to find out if there are any triggers for them. Buy a small book to keep your notes in – something that will fit in your pocket or bag so it is always handy. Make notes about what happened before each seizure. You may be able to build up a picture of when they are most likely to happen.

Most people's seizures occur without warning and for no reason. If you think yours might be triggered by something in particular, such as tiredness, it is useful to find out.

It is not true that if you have epilepsy you cannot go to discos because of the flashing lights. In fact, strobe (flashing) lights affect very few people with epilepsy and you should be able to stop any ill effects by covering one eye.

Typical triggers

These are some of the things that can trigger epileptic seizures. Knowing what sets off your seizures may help you to reduce the number you have.

- Tiredness – Lack of sleep or too many late nights can make some people more likely to have seizures. Try to stick to regular bedtimes if you can.
- Illness – Sometimes colds or sore throats can bring on a seizure.
- Missing meals – Eating a sensible diet is important for us all, including people with epilepsy. Some people find that missing meals can leave them weak and more likely to have a seizure.
- Over-excitement – Some people find that if they get too excited, or really cross or **stressed** about something, they are at greater risk of having a seizure.
- Changes in light – A few people may be affected by flashing lights, or sudden changes from light to dark or dark to light. Playing computer or video games is not usually a problem, but everyone should take a break from these every 40 minutes.

Meet Beryl and Shaun

My name is Beryl and I'm Shaun's mum. Shaun is thirteen and he has epilepsy. He did not show any signs of epilepsy until he was six. He was at primary school and he was having difficulties learning. I had noticed that he was having little absences (sort of switching off for a few moments), but I thought these were caused by the medicines he was taking for his **asthma**.

Shaun got worse and worse until he was having major **seizures**, in which he would fall down and become **unconscious**. Finally, doctors realized he had epilepsy and started him on medicines to help. Unfortunately, these weren't really of any use. He was having lots of assistance at school from extra teachers. He didn't like this because it made him different from everyone else. He also stood out like a sore thumb as he was wearing a helmet to protect him against his frequent falls, although he accepted it was necessary. We decided to try him at a special school for children with epilepsy. It was the best thing we could have done. The advantages of him being there far outweigh the disadvantages of him being away from home. He has improved so much we are absolutely amazed.

Hi. My name is Shaun. I enjoy playing football, watching television, playing computer games and going to the cinema. The real joy in my life is my collie dog, Shep. I take him for long walks on the beach near my home whenever I can.

I live at school in the week, and I go home some weekends and every holiday. I really like it here. I don't feel different like I did in my old school. Everyone else here understands what it's like to have epilepsy. I am better, too. I don't have to wear my helmet so much, only for sports or walking around, and I never wear it at home any more. I feel a lot more confident, too. I didn't used to like meeting new people, but now I am happy to.

Living with epilepsy

Everyone has different experiences of living with epilepsy. If your epilepsy is well controlled with medicines, you may find that it hardly affects your day-to-day life. If you have more serious epilepsy and you continue to have **seizures**, it may be something you have to be aware of all the time. Most people find that if they are sensible and have a positive outlook, there is no need for epilepsy to interfere with their lives too much. They say the best thing to do is concentrate on what you can do, rather than what you cannot do. That sounds like good advice, whether you have epilepsy or not!

Identity tags

Some people who have epilepsy feel more confident about going out on their own if they carry an identity card. This tells people that you have epilepsy and what they should and should not do if you have a seizure. Some people carry this information in a special identity bracelet or necklace.

The special symbol on these identity bands, bracelets and necklace tells people that you have a particular medical **condition**. It is recognized all over the world.

Being honest and open about your epilepsy can help to get rid of any wrong ideas people may have about it.

Other people

Many young people say that they can cope with the epilepsy itself. The main problem is other people. Some parents can be over-protective, stopping you from doing things for fear it might bring on a seizure. Even though you know this is only because they care, it can be difficult. Try to talk it over with them. It is important to listen to each other. If they feel that you are really taking their concerns on board, they may feel able to let up a bit.

Sometimes classmates at school get the wrong idea about epilepsy. They may assume that it means you are ill or that there are lots of things you cannot do. One boy even reported that a girl at his school refused to play with him because she thought epilepsy was **contagious** and that she would get it if she touched him! The only real way of tackling mistaken ideas like this is to explain what epilepsy is really like. Once people understand what epilepsy is (and that it is not catching), they usually forget all about it.

At school

The majority of children and young people who have epilepsy go to ordinary schools and do the same lessons, activities and homework as anyone else. If their epilepsy is well controlled with medicines, the only difference is that they may need to take a tablet at lunchtime. It is also important that teachers at school are aware that you have epilepsy, so that they know what to do in case you have a **seizure**.

Most children who have epilepsy go to ordinary schools and take part in all the school activities, just like other people.

Some children have a kind of epilepsy that cannot be so easily controlled with medicines. They may find that repeated seizures make them miss lessons, which affects their schoolwork. Frequent seizures may make it hard for them to concentrate. Some people who have epilepsy have other physical difficulties or learning problems as well. They may need some extra teaching support at school to help them achieve their full potential. Some may be happier at a special school for children with serious epilepsy, where their needs can be met more easily.

Sports for all

If your epilepsy is well controlled, there are hardly any sports you cannot try. Even if you still have seizures, you can have a go at most sports as long as you take certain precautions. The important thing is to know yourself well, to know what you feel happy doing and what is safe for you to do.

If you have epilepsy, it is perfectly safe to go swimming as long as you are with an adult who knows what to do if you have a seizure in the water.

Some people feel concerned about swimming because of the risk of drowning if a seizure happens while they are in the pool. If you have epilepsy, you should tell sports teachers and lifeguards about your **condition**. As long as they know what kind of seizures you have and what to do if you have one, you should feel safe.

Some people think that children with epilepsy should not cycle to school. For most, it is fine as long as they wear protective helmets and ride on routes away from too much traffic. Wearing a helmet is important for all cyclists – not just those who have epilepsy.

At home

For most people who have epilepsy, life at home is the same as it is for other people. Some people, who are prone to **seizures**, make a few changes around the home to help them avoid injuries when they have a seizure.

- It is best to have central heating instead of real fires, or to make sure there is always a guard in front of the fire.
- Some families fit plastic covers over any sharp edges on furniture. This reduces the risk of injury if anyone falls against them.
- If you have epilepsy, tell someone before you have a bath or shower, just in case you have a seizure while you are in water.
- It is rare for someone with epilepsy to fall out of bed if they have night-time seizures. Even so, some people feel happier if their bedroom has a low bed and a soft carpet, just in case.

If you have epilepsy it is a good idea to leave the door unlocked when you have a bath. You can always put up a sign saying that the bathroom is busy.

Take a break – holidays

People with epilepsy enjoy holidays in their own country and abroad, just like other people. If you have epilepsy, it is important to remember to pack enough medicine for your entire trip. If you are flying off on holiday, it is best to keep your supply of medicines with you in the bag you take on the plane, in case your main luggage gets lost or the flight is delayed.

If you are going abroad, you might also need to consider when to take your medicines. You probably know that when you travel to another country, you may have to alter the time on your watch. The further west or east you go, the bigger the time change there will be. This can be confusing when you are used to taking your tablets at a set time each day. Your parents or doctor should be able to help you plan when to take your medicines to adjust to such time changes.

If you have epilepsy and you are going abroad, you may need to work out a new timetable for taking your medicines. Apart from that, the only thing to remember is to enjoy your time away!

Meet Ellen

Hello, my name is Ellen. I'm eleven years old. I've got two sisters, Bethany and Kate. We've also got a family dog, Pumba, but I'm the only one who really walks him. I'm training him to do some tricks, too, but he'll only do them if he gets a biscuit for a reward and Mum says if I give him too many he'll get fat!

I've had epilepsy for more than three years now. I used to get **seizures** quite a lot. They started after I fell out of a tree that I was climbing. I was OK, except that I banged my head badly. After that I started having seizures. The world would just sort of stop and I'd feel like I wasn't really part of it for a few moments. It was really weird. Mum said I'd mumble a bit and move differently. Once it happened when I was riding my bike. I fell off and broke my arm. The doctor sent me for an **EEG**. It was a real drag while we were waiting for the EEG results because Mum was watching me like a hawk and she wouldn't even let me go out on my bike.

I got to know when a seizure was coming because I'd feel suddenly hot and a bit nervous, even if I was at home with nothing to worry about. As soon as I got a feeling like that, I'd stop what I was doing, and sit down and wait for it to pass. After the doctors decided I had epilepsy they started to give me medicine to stop the seizures. I take the tablets with a big glass of water because I'm not really very good at swallowing them. I have two tablets a day.

I've told my best friends about my epilepsy, but I haven't told anyone else in my class. It's not that I'm bothered about people knowing; it's just that there's not much point, really. Epilepsy doesn't stop me doing anything at school or at home. I do tap and jazz dance classes, I'm learning to play the piano and I like horse riding. I also like reading detective and mystery novels, and beating my friend Jess at chess!

Glossary

asthma condition in which a person's airways become narrower at times, making it difficult to breathe easily

brain control centre of the body. It controls the rest of the body and how we think, learn and feel.

condition physical complaint that is not a disease or an illness – usually a long-term problem

contagious when a disease is contagious, it can be passed on to other people by the person who has it. Epilepsy is not a disease or an illness and it is certainly not contagious.

diagnose when a doctor decides what disease or condition a person has

EEG stands for electroencephollogram (you say 'electro-enkefalo-gram'). An EEG test checks the activity of electrical signals in the brain.

electrical signals messages made of electricity, one of the commonest forms of energy

infection kind of disease that can be caught from other people. The most common infectious disease is the cold.

meningitis illness that causes the membranes (skin) covering a person's brain to become inflamed, which sometimes can cause damage to the brain

nerve cells tiny bundles of fibres that transmit information between the different parts of the brain

nerve endings group of nerves at certain points of our body, such as the ends of our fingers

nerves parts of the body that take messages to and from the brain with information from our five senses (sight, sound, touch, hearing and smell)

seizures change in behaviour caused by a temporary change in the way nerve cells in the brain work. There are many different kinds of seizures (sometimes called 'fits'), from the kind that cause you to fall down and shake uncontrollably to the kind where you simply 'switch off' for a few seconds and appear to be daydreaming.

side-effects unwanted reactions to a medicine that you take. Usually an epilepsy medicine helps to reduce seizures, but may make you feel sleepy or sick. These are unwanted side-effects.

spinal cord part of the body that links the brain to the nerves all around the body. It is protected by the backbone.

stress what someone feels when they worry a lot about something, such as a test or an exam

trigger something that sets off (causes) a seizure in a person who has epilepsy

unconscious when someone is not conscious, they are not aware of where they are or what they are doing. They are not asleep, but they are not awake either.

Helpful books and addresses

BOOKS

Body Systems, Thinking and Feeling, Angela Royston, Heinemann Library, 1997

I Have Epilepsy, Althea, Dinosaur Publications, 1991

Epilepsy – The Detective's Story, Peter Rogan and David Hollomby, Roby.

The Illustrated Junior Encyclopaedia of Epilepsy, Dr Richard Appleton, Roby.

WEBSITE

www.epilepsy.org.uk/kids

ORGANIZATIONS

British Epilepsy Association is a charity that supports people who have epilepsy. You can contact them at:
Anstey House
Gate Way Drive
Yeadon, Leeds LS19 7XY
Telephone: 0113 210 8800
Freephone helpline: 0808 800 5050
Fax: 0113 391 0300
E-mail: epilepsy@bea.org.uk
Website: www.epilepsy.org.uk

The National Centre for Young People With Epilepsy (NCYPE)
provides specialized services for young people with epilepsy in the UK.
St Piers Lane
Lingfield, Surrey RH7 6PW
Telephone: 01342 832243
Fax: 01342 834939
E-mail: info@ncype.org.uk
Website: www.ncype.org.uk

IN AUSTRALIA

Epilepsy Foundation of Victoria
818 Burke Road, Camberwell
Victoria 3124
Australia
Telephone: 1800 134 087
Fax: 03 9882 7159
E-mail: epilepsy@epilepsy.asn.au

The Epilepsy Association
Suite 6 'Oxford Place'
44–46 Oxford Street
Epping NSW 2121
Telephone: 1300 366 162
Fax: 02 9869 4122
E-mail: epilepsy@epilepsy.org.au
Website: mfalson@epilepsy.org.au

Index

blood tests 11
brain 6, 7, 8, 10

causes of epilepsy 10
check-ups 16
computer and video games 19
controlling epilepsy 14–15

diagnosis 10, 11

EEG 11, 28
electrical signals 7, 11
exercise and sports 15, 25

healthy diet 15
holidays 27
home life 26–7

identity cards, bracelets and
    necklaces 22
illness 10, 19

kind and number of seizures 5, 8

light, changes in 19
living with epilepsy 22–3

meals, missing 19
medicines 4, 5, 13, 14, 15, 16–17,
    18, 20, 22, 24, 27, 29
mistaken ideas about epilepsy 23

nerve cells 6, 7, 11
nerves and nerve endings 6

over-excitement 19

people affected by epilepsy 4
protective helmets 20, 21, 25

safety measures 26
school 20, 21, 23, 24–5
seizures 4, 5, 6, 7, 8, 9, 10, 12, 14,
    15, 18, 19, 20, 22, 24, 25, 26,
    28, 29
shaking 9, 12
special schools 20, 21, 24
spinal cord 6
stress 15, 19
strobe (flashing) lights 19
swimming 25

tests for epilepsy 11, 13
tiredness 19
trigger diary 18
triggers 14, 18–19

unconsciousness 5, 8, 9, 20

what to do when a seizure
    happens 9